The Gover

WITHDRAWN

Other Books by Matthew David Brozik and Jacob Sager Weinstein

The Government Manual for New Superheroes
The Government Manual for New Wizards

The Government Manual

for

NEW PIRATES

Matthew David Brozik and Jacob Sager Weinstein

**Andrews McMeel
Publishing, LLC**

Kansas City

The Government Manual for New Pirates

07 08 09 10 11 MLT 10 9 8 7 6 5 4 3 2 1

ISBN-13: 978-0-7407-6790-6
ISBN-10: 0-7407-6790-9

Library of Congress Control Number: 2006937594

www.andrewsmcmeel.com

Avast, Schools and Businesses

Andrews McMeel books are available at quantity discounts with bulk purchase
for educational, business, or sales promotional use. For information,
please write to: Special Sales Department, Andrews McMeel Publishing, LLC,
4520 Main Street, Kansas City, Missouri 64111.

Dedication

With love as strong as rum—and none o' that watered-down grog stuff—this book be dedicated to Lauren Sager Weinstein (who be holdin' the treasure map to one of our hearts) and Wade Brozik and Adam Brozik (who be two of the scurviest knaves ye'll ever be meetin').

Acknowledgments

The Brotherhood be hoistin' the naval flag of gratitude to these hearty souls what sailed with us:

Robert "Shepbeard" Shepard

Lane Butler, Scourge of Kansas City

Calico Christina Schafer

The Pirate King be grateful to S. "Robbin'-some" Kutner and Sheryl "Danger" Zohn, what read the manuscript and made a-sure it be right and true.

Contents

CHAPTER THREE
SPEAK IN THE MANNER OF A PIRATE   23

CHAPTER FOUR
SAIL YE LIKE A PIRATE   39

TREASURE! 89

Avast, Reader!

by Calico Jack, King of the Pirates

If ye be a landlubber, ye be askin' yerself, "Why
would the Government publish a manual for pirates?
Goodness me—surely the Government doesn't sanc-
tion such a scandalous activity!" And then, most
likely, ye be polishin' your monocle, and mincin'
around yer dry, salt-free mansion, or whatever it be
that ye landlubbers do when ye aren't makin' trouble
for honest pirates like meself.

But if ye be of the Brotherhood . . . why, then,
ye know the answer already. The radish-eatin' *land*
Government don't dare publish no manual for us, no,
but the *Pirate* Government got no such qualms.

Ye see, sometime aback, just when me crew was
about to board a fat Spanish galleon, a-drippin' with
rubies and doubloons, up speaks Jonesy the cabin
boy—a green lad, barely tall enough for his head to
reach his hat. "Dibs on the booty," says he.

"Dibs," says he!

A billion blisterin' barnacles on a drowned man's beard! There be no "dibs" in piratin'. Booty be divided among the crew, from the lowest deck-swabber to the highest masthand. So says the Pirate Code, and so says I, and I'll run through any scurvy dog what says different.

So after I finished runnin' Jonesy through, I set me to thinkin'. What with the land bein' so crowded, and the sea bein' so free, there's more joinin' the sweet trade than the Brotherhood can teach. "May be," says I, "we need a book what can teach the young 'uns how to pirate like men. May be," says I, "we need a *manual*."

Course, not I nor me men be much for readin' or writin', unless it be readin' or writin' treasure maps. But we be old hands at findin' booty, be it gold or be it flesh. So we set to findin' us some human booty. We be raidin' libraries and universities, honor societies and debatin' clubs, until we get us a real, honest-to-God writin' man, what knows all the letters and most of the words, and we set to teachin' him the ways of the Brethren. And now—of his own free will, mind ye—he's written this here manual what ye hold in yer own two hands, or yer own two hooks, as may be.

Aye, he don't speak the pirate tongue. He's always endin' words with a *g* what ought be endin' with one of them apostrophes. But he writes sound and true, and he knows the Code from stem to stern.

So if ye be wantin' to join the sovereign kingdom of the lawless seas, then read ye this manual, or kidnap yerself a fancy Lady and have her read it to ye.

Arrrrr!

Calico Jack
King of the Pirates

CHAPTER ONE

WHERE BE PIRATES?

Finding Your Brethren

If you have purchased this book, you have already demonstrated your desire to join the fast-growing field of piracy. You have also demonstrated your complete inaptitude for it. Please put this book down at once.

However, if you have *stolen* this book, you are off to an excellent start. The following pages will teach you much of what you need to know to develop your natural instinct for dishonesty into a thriving career.

But a book can only teach you so much. There will come a time when you must learn, firsthand, from flesh-and-blood members of the Brotherhood. For one thing, you will need to hear the pirate tongue spoken, to improve your accent. Also, of course, piracy is not a field practiced in solitude. Even if you know everything you must know, you will still need to find other pirates to give you an entry-level job as a cabin boy, in addition to an entry-level parrot and perhaps an entry-level tattoo.

Your first act as a buccaneer, therefore, will be to seek out others of your kind, and then to conk them on the head with a tankard of grog to show them that you mean business. (For more on traditional greetings, see chapter 3.) But where will you find your fellow seafaring rogues?

We Sail the Ocean Blue

Scientists tell us that the earth is two-thirds water, and that water (at least on the surface) is three-eighths pirates. You need only set sail from any port, and before long your ship will encounter (and, perhaps, be boarded and sunk by) a hearty band of buccaneers.

If you wish to speed up the process considerably, you would do well to set sail toward the most pirate-populated region on earth: the Caribbean.

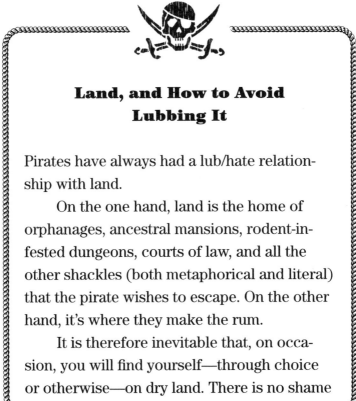

Land, and How to Avoid Lubbing It

Pirates have always had a lub/hate relationship with land.

On the one hand, land is the home of orphanages, ancestral mansions, rodent-infested dungeons, courts of law, and all the other shackles (both metaphorical and literal) that the pirate wishes to escape. On the other hand, it's where they make the rum.

It is therefore inevitable that, on occasion, you will find yourself—through choice or otherwise—on dry land. There is no shame in this, as long as you remember the following tips:

Always stay within smelling distance of seawater. In the pirate cosmos a small island is better than a big one, and a beach is better than a town. In a worst-case scenario, if you find yourself in a large, inland city, locate the nearest aquarium as soon as possible.

If you fall in love with the governor's pretty daughter, kidnap her at once and bring her back to your ship. Do not allow her delicate feminine charms to lure you into a respectable life.

Ensure that any drinking establishments you visit are suitable for a member of the Brotherhood. If, upon opening the front door, you see a quiet, smoke-free establishment, decorated in neutral tones and with potted plants, flee at once. By contrast, if opening the front door reveals a packed house of drunken, bearded, tattooed men smoking pipes and slugging one another, you may relax. If you do not need to open the door at all because, as you approach, a drunken, bearded, tattooed man is knocked backward through it, shattering it into splinters, that is even better.

The Caribbean

The Caribbean has been a favored stomping ground of pirates for centuries. Its favorable currents provide the means to swiftly overtake unsuspecting ships. Its countless secluded coves provide safe harbors to hide in after capturing one of those ships. Its sandy beaches provide ample burying ground for treasure while the ship is hiding in one of those coves. And the comely wenches provide countless reasons not to bother overtaking those unsuspecting ships in the first place.

Among the region's seven thousand islands, a few locations are particular favorites for pirates.

Tortuga

What Jerusalem is to devotees of the world's three major religions, Tortuga is to pirates, except that pirates view the constant violence in their homeland as a wholly positive thing. A lawless, decadent mass of groghouses and brothels, with drunken or otherwise unconscious bodies of pirates littering every street corner, Tortuga is—in the words of the island's official motto—"The most wretched hive of scum and villainy you'll ever find!"

Tortuga consistently takes the top spot in *Pirate News & World Report*'s "favorite places" poll.

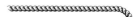

Best-Loved Tortuga Shops
and Restaurants

House o' Wenches

Rummy's Rum Shack

House o' Rum

Black Jack's Blackjacks and Blunt
    Instruments

One-Eyed Mac's Old-Fashioned Rum-Soaked
    Wenchery

I Can't Believe It Be Not Rum!

Hispaniola

Not too far from Tortuga lies Hispaniola, which for
many years failed to achieve the popularity of its
neighbor, despite an advertising campaign boasting,
"We're number two in scum and villainy—but we try
harder."

Recently, Hispaniola has found more success marketing itself as an upscale alternative for the discriminating pirate. Offering specialty rum from its fine microdistilleries and specialty wenches from its fine microbrothels, the island is rapidly becoming a favorite destination for young, unlawful, but polished pirates, or "yuppies."

If you choose to visit, be warned: In an effort to preserve the exclusive air of Hispaniola, its citizens recently voted to make pronouncing the "H" a plank-walkable offense.

Favorite Hispaniola Shops and Restaurants

Starbucks

Other Caribbean Hot Spots

There are more pirate-friendly islands in the Caribbean than could possibly be listed in this volume. However, the experienced buccaneer will soon develop the instincts to predict what sort of reception he will receive, based purely on an island's name. As a rule, the more unappealing a name is to anybody else, the more homey and inviting it will sound to a gentleman o' fortune.

Cockroach Island, Backstabbers Bay, and Dead Chest Key all have large pirate populations. Rainbowpony Cove does not.

Ice Pirates

Where there is water, there are pirates sailing upon it—even if that water is frozen.

The Ice Pirates of Antarctica are not as well known as their Caribbean counterparts, but they are no less feared by those who have encountered them. Like all pirates, they spend their days sailing, and their nights drinking and carousing. Of course, at the poles, this means six straight months of sailing without rest, followed by six straight months of nonstop drinking and carousing. At the beginning of polar piracy season, members of the Antarctic Brotherhood are still recovering from the most powerful hangovers known to man, and by its end, the crews are so sleep-deprived that their massive ice frigates can easily be sunk by stray icebergs or penguins. But during that narrow window when they suffer from neither headaches nor exhaustion, Frostbeard and his men are the terrors of the tundra, bringing in haul after haul of precious whale blubber and gleaming icicles. Indeed, nothing strikes fear in the heart of an Eskimo like the sight of a rapidly approaching sled flying the skull and crossbones, pulled by a team of peg-legged, eye patch–wearing huskies.

Chapter Two

LOOK YE LIKE A PIRATE

No Slave to Fashion Be Ye

It would be ironic indeed if a seafaring adventurer, after turning his back on the confining laws of the land-bound masses, took pains to dress according to their fads and fashions. In any case, a real pirate cares little for outward appearance; true piracy comes from within.

That said, you will acquire most of your garments by stealing them from law-abiding citizens, and you might, from time to time, find yourself wearing clothes that are disturbingly clean, pleasant-smelling, and free of holes.

Fear not. After just a few days at sea, exposed to the brutal heat, the rank odors, the salty water, and all the other severe conditions of your body (and, to a lesser extent, your vessel), your attire will lose its garishness and its gimcrackery. In fact, like men themselves, only the heartiest of raiment will survive the pirate's life. The unsubstantial stuff—the lace, the linen, the muslin, the silk—will not last long enough to make swabs for the deck.

Necessary Items

As noted, the pirate is not generally concerned with how he looks. The following accoutrements have become de rigueur, therefore, not for aesthetic but rather for practical piratical reasons.

Head Covering

The deservedly infamous Pirates of Pittsburgh are not the only members of the Brotherhood to wear hats as a matter of course while on duty.* A hat or

* Though they might be the only ones to wear matching caps, not to mention colorful caps with a logo.

other head covering keeps the glaring sun off one's head during daylight hours and keeps one's noggin warm the rest of the time. It is also an excellent place for hiding small amounts of treasure when you do not have access to shovels and a beach.

Once, the so-called *bicorner* hat was very popular, in part because one needed not worry overmuch about putting it on properly—as long as the corners were to the sides, "front" and "back" were of no moment. Still, there were enough pirates for whom even that was too difficult, prompting, eventually, the advent of the even more popular *tricorner* hat.

Alternatively, you could just wear a scarf.

Beard

The beard is a functional facial accessory. As your eyebrows keep the literal sweat of your brow (see above) out of your eyes (see below), your beard will keep the sweat of your cheeks and chin out of your mouth and off your neck. At the same time, you can store in your beard rations—trout jerky, hardtack, lime wedges—for those times when you can't get to the galley, such as when you are on watch in the crow's-nest. Finally, a beard can serve as a rough indicator of a pirate's age and sex.

Eye Patch(es)

At one time, eye patches were worn only when a man had lost an eye and wanted to keep his brain from being exposed to the elements and rotting.

Now, however, the eye patch is more symbol than safeguard. This might seem to contradict the rule that pirate dress is based on practicality rather than appearance. After all, wearing a patch over a working eye significantly limits one's ability to see, and completely destroys one's depth perception, making it difficult if not impossible to tell whether that Coast Guard cutter or sea monster is several leagues away or just off the port bow (or, for that matter, whether it is a Coast Guard cutter or a sea monster in the first place, the proper response to each being different*).

* Unless, of course, the Coast Guard cutter is the U.S.S. *Sea Monster*.

Remember, though, that a pirate's greatest weapon is his reputation. If you are sufficiently fearsome, your victims will surrender before you have fired a single shot (or swung a single cutlass), allowing you all the more time to enjoy the items that recently belonged to them. Your eye patch sends your foes a message of extreme bravado, indicating that you are willing to take on all comers with one arm tied behind your back, or, more literally, one eye tied behind your patch. (Note: Wearing two eye patches will not make you seem twice as fearsome, and might in fact interfere with your navigational duties.)

You should alternate daily which eye your patch covers, to avoid lasting weakness in either one and uneven tanning.

Tattoos

Although reading and writing are pastimes for landlubbers (as are arithmetic, regular bathing, brushing one's teeth, eating with utensils, chewing with one's mouth closed, badminton, opera, and not pushing people off wooden planks into shark-infested waters), nonetheless many pirates choose to be "inked," often in words.

Popular tattoos include the names of favored wenches (Mary, Rosemary, Maryann); endorsements of highly rated pirate-friendly establishments (Mary's Alehouse, Rosemary's Bawdy House, Maryann's Brothel and Breakfast, Wendy's); and last wills and/or testaments ("To me most favored wench, Marie, I leave me antique snuffbox, me second-best cutlass, and all me tattoos, includin' this one, if she be able to get 'em off me corpse.").

Some pirates have treasure maps tattooed on their bodies. The pirate considering this option should select an expanse of skin as free of moles as possible, to avoid the unfortunate fate of Spotty Pete, who spent the last decade of his life on a fruitless hunt for Melanoma Isle.

Hooks and Pegs

Hooks and pegs are not, of course, mandatory for all pirates—merely those missing hands or legs. Specifically, hooks replace hands and pegs replace legs. Replacing your hand with a peg will make it hard to slide down a taut rigging in the heat of battle, and replacing your leg with a hook will make it hard to put your pants on.

Earrings and Other Jewelry

Real men wear jewelry—finger rings and earrings especially. Adorning oneself liberally with gold and silver isn't pretentiousness but pragmatism: Precious metals, after all, are best kept close at hand, assuming you have hands. (If you have hooks, you will notice that a large gold ring will tend to slip right off. Consider getting large gold hooks, or several very small gold rings.)

Precious metals also serve as a meter of a pirate's mettle. Gold earrings, for example, symbolize a successful voyage around the notoriously treacherous Cape Horn. Gold nose rings represent a successful voyage through the Sound of Bull Horn. Gold teeth represent a string of successful voyages without a toothbrush.

Items of jewelry singularly unpopular among pirates include leg irons and rope chokers.

Parrots

Parrots have a number of different characteristics that endear them to pirates. All 350 different species of bird in the order of parrots are zygodactyls, having the four toes on each foot placed two in front and two in back, an evolutionary advantage making it easy for them to perch on a pirate's shoulder. Also, unlike other pets, parrots can be taught to curse.

Even those parrots who do not pick up a salty vocabulary from their owners liven up many a dull hour at sea with their calls of "Dead men tell no tales!" or "Polly be wantin' a cracker!" And a parrot's ability to parrot is not limited to human speech; the bird who can convincingly imitate the sound of a cannon's report can save his owner's life when ammo runs low.

Although the popularity of parrots as pets has led to a thriving and often illegal trade in the birds, pirates themselves have chosen not to participate in it, mainly because they can't figure out what to wear on their shoulders while doing so.

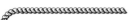

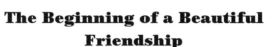

The Beginning of a Beautiful Friendship

Among the many reasons why parrots are popular among pirates, the most historically significant is simply that *parrot* sounds a lot like *pirate*, especially to a pirate (or a parrot) who has been up late drinking. Thus it was that when the famed Captain Henry Morgan, fairly flammable with spiced rum, issued orders to his second-in-command to enlarge their boat's crew complement, he returned to the vessel to find it instead transformed into a veritable aviary, and a tradition was born.

Teeth

Teeth are optional for a pirate.

Not Recommended

A pirate may wear a tuxedo under precious few circumstances, none of which will be described here, and in any event never before six in the evening.

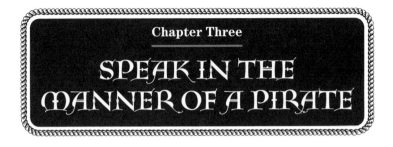

Chapter Three

SPEAK IN THE MANNER OF A PIRATE

Rough Waters Ahead?

You will soon see that this chapter contains many more tables and charts than the previous ones. Studies indicate that in populations with a distaste for book learning (a group that certainly includes pirates, both current and aspiring), tables and charts are 342% more intimidating than any other form of knowledge, except statistics (which are 456% more intimidating than average) and lengthy compound sentences (no intimidation rating currently available).

A Very Complex and Intimidating Statistical Equation

A pirate's fear of book learning can even cause him to skip whole sidebars when it appears that they will contain excessive scientific or mathematical language. We may demonstrate this logically by letting Q = Fear of Book Learning and Y = Excessive Mathematical Language. If we then take the square of the derivative of the cosine of the tangent of the HELP! I am an honest literary man being forced to write this book against my will! Please contact the Governor of St. Thomas Island, the Head Constable of St. Thomas Island, and the President of the St. Thomas Island Book Club and Literary Debating Society at once. Thank you. Thus, we can see that $\int yx \, \frac{q^2}{z} = \sqrt{\coprod_{Q}^{q} 5}$.

You might therefore find it helpful to view the various charts and tables in a more pirate-friendly light: as navigation charts (through the tempestuous seas of grammar) or as treasure maps (to the precious booty of clear communication.)

Or you can just skip to chapter 4.

Conjugation

The most important verb in the pirate tongue is *to be*. Master its use, and you will be a long way toward speaking fluent Pirate. For your convenience, here is a chart of the most commonly used conjugations of *to be*. Clip it out and carry it with you until you have memorized it, lest you make an embarrassing (and potentially fatal) grammatical misstep.

Once you have memorized the forms of *to be*, you can use them to conjugate any other verb. For example, if you wish to use the third-person subjunctive of the verb *to yammer*, you would simply say *be yammerin'*. If, however, you wish to use the second-person familiar future tense,

	Present	Past	Future	Subjunctive	Pluperfective Nominative
First Person	be	be	be	be	be
Second Person Formal ("Ye")	be	be	be	be	be
Second Person Familiar ("Ya")	be	be	be	be	be
Third Person Plural	be	be	be	be	be
First Parrot Singular	be	be	be	be	be

you would say *be yammerin'*. The third-person pluperfective nominative would be *be yammerin'*, and so forth.

Readers who are unable to extrapolate further might wish to purchase (or steal, during a raid on a bookshop or bookship) the handy reference work *500 Verbs What I Be Conjugatin' in the Pirate Tongue*.

A Pirate's Alphabet: More Than Just X

Every tar worth his salt—and vice versa—knows that *X* is far and away the most useful of all the letters; it is, after all, *X* and no other letter that marks the spot. But there are other letters as well—many others, in fact—and some of them have merit in their own right. (Note: This list is intended to be illustrative only, not exhaustive. No single list could include all possible letters.)

C   A pirate needs to get the daily recommended allowance of this vitamin, lest he become a scurvy knave.

D The lowest passing grade on the Pirate/
Swashbuckler Aptitude Test (PSAT).

H On buoys, indicates that a pirate hospital is
nearby, either on an island or a sterile barge.

O Shorthand for "hug," often used on ransom
notes, in the closing salvo just above the
signature.

R When in a circle, indicates registered
trademark status of your name, e.g.: Captain
Carbuncle®; Jim the Putrescent®; Planky®.

Absence Makes the Boat Go Faster

Perhaps more important than the letters pirates use
are the letters they do *not* use—which is most of
them, at one time or another. Where a land dweller
might say, "I should like to purchase a halfpenny's
worth of gunpowder for musket-loading purposes,
please," a pirate would say, "A ha'penn'orth o'
po'der fer the loadin'." Thanks to this conversational
efficiency, in the time it takes a land dweller to make

his request, the pirate will already have finished his transaction, loaded his musket, kidnapped the land dweller's daughter, and set sail. It is no coincidence that the only natural enemies of pirates are those who speak even less than they do: ninjas and (under certain circumstances) monks.

If you are unsure which letters to omit when speaking Pirate, just remember this handy rule of thumb: If a letter appears at the beginning of a word or at the end, you may safely drop it. Likewise if it appears anywhere in between.

Some Selected Definitions of Some Selected Pirate Words

Ahoy. Greetings. Also used in onboard gambling activities, where the phrase "Chips ahoy!" means "Show me the money!"

Arr. The most versatile word in a pirate's vocabulary. It can mean "Yes," "No," "Uh-oh," "Prepare to die," or (in certain very specific circumstances) "The brown one second from the left, but not the blue one, unless it is Tuesday."

Avast. When used as an imperative verb, signifies "stop," as in "Avast there, landlubber." When used as an adjective, it signifies something of such great size that the speaker cannot pause for breath when describing it, as in "Avast canyon."

Davy Jones's locker. (1) The place to which all pirates must ultimately go. The infinite sea at the end of the plank of life. The final keelhauling. The great groghouse in the sky. (2) The place where Davy Jones keeps his postcards of scantily clad wenches. (Note: only applicable if there is a pirate on board named Davy Jones.)

Grog. Rum; especially rum mixed with hot water and flavored. Just as Eskimos have hundreds of words for snow, so pirates have hundreds of words for rum. (The Ice Pirates of Antarctica, it should be noted, have several hundred words for rum-flavored sno-cones.)

Scurvy dog. A biting insult, unless your captain combines a fondness for pets with a disdain for citrus.

Wench. A woman.

Winch. A windlass turned by a crank. (Note: Confusing *wench* and *winch* can cause considerable embarrassment at pirate social events.)

A [Large Number] [Gerund] [Plural Noun] on a(n) [Adjective] [Noun]!

Now that you have learned the words of the pirate tongue, you will want to combine them into phrases. Sometimes, you will use these phrases to cajole, to urge, to praise, or to thank. Mostly, though, you will use them to curse.

Please note that pirate cursing does *not* involve the utterance of obscene words. Gentlemen o' fortune might roam the lawless seas, burning towns to the ground, sinking ships, and assaulting innocent citizens with cannon and cutlass, but they do have manners.

As a result, pirate cursing demands considerable inventiveness and creativity. Indeed, cursing may be the most exquisite of all pirate art forms, surpassing even scrimshaw and tobacco spitting. The famed Pirate Curse-Off—held annually in an undisclosed location on an unrevealed date—draws connoisseurs from across the globe. Organizers of the most recent of these events estimated attendance at "five hundred flea-feedin' seadogs on a rickety wood bench," up from the previous year's "three hundred lice-scratchin' lunkheads in a salt-stinkin' saloon."

With practice, you, too, can learn this art. Perhaps you will even attain a level of mastery like that of the notorious Red Rackham, who—as he stood on the gallows—took advantage of an obscure law forbidding the hanging of a pirate in mid-curse and launched into a single interjection of such length and complexity that he was able to delay his execution by a full twenty-four hours. At that point (as he triumphantly uttered the concluding words "and your second cousin as well!") he dropped dead of exhaustion, making his triumph over the hangman complete.

Until you reach that level of skill, when you need to express surprise, anger, affection, or any other emotion, simply refer to the following table. Select one phrase from each column, and you will have an impressive exclamation for any occasion.

Number	Adjective	Noun	Prepositional Phrase	Adjective	Noun
A billion	blisterin'	barnacles	on a	bilious blue	beard!
Ten thousand	thunderin'	typhoons	on a	dead man's	bialy!
A couple	smolderin'	monkeys	on a	drowned man's	bottle of rum!
Gazillions of	rottin'	corpses	on a	scurvy dog's	chest!
6.02×10^{23}	vivisectin'	fo'c'sles	in the general vicinity of a	Spaniard's	cutlass!
No fewer than 12 but no more than 16	dashin'	red balloons	on a	poorly maintained	bootstrap!

Skullcaps and Crossbones

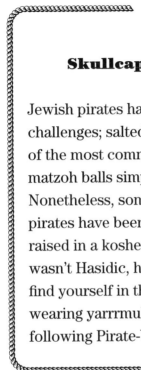

Jewish pirates have always faced special challenges; salted pork, for example, is one of the most common foods at sea, and salted matzoh balls simply do not travel as well. Nonetheless, some of history's greatest pirates have been Jewish. Jean Lafitte was raised in a kosher home, and if Blackbeard wasn't Hasidic, he certainly looked it. If you find yourself in the company of buccaneers wearing yarrrmulkes, you might find the following Pirate-Yiddish dictionary useful.

Common Pirate Expression	Yiddish Equivalent
Scurvy dog	*Fershlugginer momzer*
Arr	*Oy*
Arrrrrr	*Oy vey*
Arrrrrrrrrrrrrr	*Oy vey is mir*
Avast	Enough already
Gentleman o' fortune	*Gonif*
Six sheets t' the wind	*Shikker*
Arr! Next time that bilious, backstabbin' bilge rat captures ten fat galleons a-drippin' with gold, may he choke t' death on every stinkin' doubloon!	*Oy! Tsen shifn mit geld zol er farmorgn, un dos gantse gelt zol er farkrenkn!*

Talk Like a Landlubber Day

Each year on September 19, pirates all around the world observe International Talk Like a Landlubber Day. If you wish to participate but have forgotten the landlubber tongue, there is no need to worry. Simply read this chapter in reverse.

Chapter Four

SAIL YE LIKE A PIRATE

Choosing Your Ship

You now know how to dress the part and how to curse. To complete your sea change into a pirate, all you need to do now is go to sea.

That is, all you need to do now is go to sea *in a boat.*

Not just any boat, of course. A pirate's ship must be swift, sturdy, and well equipped. She must have the agility to overtake your victims' vessels and to outrun authority, the fortitude to withstand bombardment, and the wherewithal to return fire. Your ship should also have an anchor and either a lot of sails or some kind of motor. A paddlewheel is not appropriate unless you plan to terrorize only the Mississippi River, as did the legendary Hucklebeard (and his comely consort, Buccaneer "Bucky" Thatcher).

We shall consider the actual sailing of your vessel in greater detail below. For now it will suffice that you have a ship of some variety and that it is more inclined to float than to sink. Find yourself a bottle of rum, for it is time to christen your ship.*

Naming Your Ship

For reasons unclear and buried too deep in history to be found, questioned, and drawn and quartered, it is a nautical tradition to name ships with puns. The custom shows no signs of letting up, and an unplayful vessel name is viewed as an invitation for immediate boarding, raiding, and scuttling. Some pirates will even rename a ship before sinking her.

---

* In fact, the phrase "Find yourself a bottle of rum" should be understood to precede every instruction in this book.

Another intractable tradition is that a ship is referred to as "she" or "her" no matter how unfeminine (or positively masculine) its name. Thus the famed Captain Mad Mudlark was often heard to remark, "*Pegleg Joe's Festerin' Carcass*? She be a beauty, and I be lovin' her!"

When you have chosen a name for your ship and have had that name stenciled upon her hull in a fearsome font with waterproof paint, take your bottle of rum in hand. Open your bottle of rum. Drink the contents of your bottle of rum. Then smash the empty bottle on the fore of your ship. If your ship goes down at this point, begin reading this chapter again.

Good Names for a Pirate Ship

- *Blood Vessel*
- *Death Merchant Marine*
- *Craft Unfair*
- *A Painful Berth*
- *I Keel You*
- *The Black Catamaran*
- H.M.S. *Parasite*
- *The Bad Ship Lollipop*

Bad Names for a Pirate Ship

- *Sea Student*
- *The Dingy Dinghy*
- *Idle Warship*
- *Grim Rowboat*
- *Kraken Jokes*
- *Holey Scow*
- H.M.S. *Parasol*
- *The Love Boat*

Assembling Your Crew

Unless you plan to emulate the fiercely independent Freebeard, captain—and crew—of the *Lone Shark*, you will need to enlist or impress other pirates to man your man-o'-war.

The large pirating firms use a program of internships coordinated with accredited pirate schools to woo the best young student pirates into their employ. Typically, a senior associate pirate will tour tropical-island-based institutions of higher hijacking education, meeting one-on-one with those at the top of their class in Looting, Cursing, Drinking, Orienteering and Cartography, Wenching, and Parrot Care. He will then report back to the Recruiting Committee, which will consider the résumés of the best and brigandest and invite those it thinks have the most qualifications and fewest qualms to join ranks for a season. If a particular young pirate fits in well with the established crew—if he can hold his rum and his chantey-singing is in harmony—he might be invited to join permanently, sometimes with an offer of a generous signing booty.

You, on the other hand, will want to visit a tavern or brothel nearest wherever your new ship is docked, grab the first ten or twenty breathing men you see, and bring them aboard under cover of night, setting sail before they regain consciousness. When they do, and you are already some six hundred miles from land, you can make introductions over grog, compare tattoos, and divvy up duties, including those involved in the sailing of your ship, which will be discussed below.

Know Your Ship

Familiarity with the basics of vessel structure and function are assumed. This section will discuss those parts of a boat of particular interest to a pirate.

Keel

A shipbuilder will tell you that the *keel* is the longitudinal structure along the centerline at the bottom of a vessel's hull. A pirate will tell you that the keel is the part of the boat where you keelhaul somebody—that is, where you tie him to the bottom of the boat and drag him underwater as punishment for mutiny, or for defining *keel* using fancy, book-learned words that make the captain feel stupid. (For this reason, shipbuilders shun face-to-face contact with pirates, preferring to communicate via letters written from a safe distance and—if possible— dictated by semaphore from a safer distance still.)

Masts

The *masts* are the tall structures that carry your sail or sails. Eventually, you will learn to distinguish among foremasts, mainmasts, topmasts, mizzenmasts, and royal masts. In the meantime, you need only know that you can lash mutineers to any of them.

Plank

The *plank* is a long, thin, flat piece of timber extended outward from the side of a ship, upon which mutineers and other prisoners are forced to walk, over (and, thence, into) shark-infested waters. (Unless the mutiny has been successful; in that case, it is the captain who does the walking.)

Brig

The *brig* is the prison on a ship. It is where you will put someone while you decide whether to keelhaul him, lash him to one or more masts, or make him walk the plank.

Cannons

Your ship's *cannons* are its principal devices for inflicting harm upon others from a distance. (If you have strapped a mutineer to the muzzle of a cannon, this distance will be very short indeed.)

The term *loose cannon*, in the sense of an unpredictable or uncontrolled person who is likely to cause unintentional damage, derives directly from nautico-piratical experience, specifically the not-uncommon occurrence of a loaded and primed cannon becoming dislodged from its station on a tossing ship in the midst of battle. Likewise, the term *cannonization* refers to making a saint of an unpredictable or uncontrolled person by firing him from a ship into the great wide ocean.

All Aboard

Which of the following does not belong with the others: *starboard, larboard, aboveboard, overboard, shuffleboard*?

The answer is *aboveboard. Starboard* is a nautical term for the side of a ship on the right when one is facing forward. *Larboard* is another word for *port*, or the left side of a ship. *Overboard* is where those who have worn out their welcome aboard go. And *shuffleboard*, of course, is a boon to pirates everywhere: It is often while cruise-ship passengers are playing shuffleboard that pirates steal their things.

Aboveboard should not be in a pirate's vocabulary.

Dangers of the Deep

The oceans are not just vast—providing a seemingly limitless area on which you stalk your victims and hide from the authorities—but also unfathomably deep, providing an almost limitless volume in which menacing creatures will be invisible to you until they are summoned or disturbed or simply grow peckish.

Chief among the dangers of the deep are sharks and killer whales, sirens, the Kraken, and Godzilla.

Sharks and Killer Whales

Most sharks are predatory, although the largest kinds feed on plankton, which itself is sufficient reason not to name your vessel the *Plankton*. However, sharks and pirates have long enjoyed a symbiotic existence, with pirates providing food for sharks in the form of those ejected forcibly from pirate vessels, and sharks providing the service of destroying evidence of the same.

Killer whales are more highly organized—and, therefore, even more dangerous—than sharks. In fact, killer whales demonstrate an ability to work together that far surpasses that of any pirate crew, in large part because killer whales do not drink rum.

Sirens

Winged, winsome, and wily, the legendary sirens sang to lure unwary sailors to their doom upon rocks. Named for these mythical creatures, modern-day mechanical sirens will alert the unwary pirate that his ship is being approached by Coast Guard cutters and that the time is nigh to raise sails and make away.

The Kraken

The Kraken is an enormous sea monster said to appear off the coast of Norway. There are only two accounts of sailors encountering the Kraken and living to tell about it.

The first comes from the very fortunate Captain Alfred, erstwhile Pirate Laureate and sole survivor of the wreck of the *Lady of Shalott*. According to Alfred, the Kraken will be seen only once by man, when the world is consumed by the flames of Armageddon. Captain Alfred was reportedly fond of telling his crew stories at bedtime, and his crewmen were reportedly fond of throwing themselves overboard.

The second account comes from a group of sailors who claim to have met, and defeated, Davy Jones himself, in a ramshackle adventure involving not merely the Kraken but a magical compass and an undead monkey. They are not considered plausible witnesses.

Godzilla

The tales told of Godzilla are legion. The result of extreme mutation caused by nuclear testing, this thirty-story-tall monster breathes fire and has a spiked tail like a combination mace and battering ram. Godzilla lives underwater—exactly where is unknown—but, to the relief of seafarers at large, prefers to wreak havoc on land, and particularly in the Orient. To be safe nonetheless, you might want to avoid trafficking in raw fish, for which Godzilla has repeatedly demonstrated a fondness. Also, even if you get wind of great treasure buried there, steer clear of Monster Island, where Godzilla and his friends summer.

The Importance of
Proper Sailing Technique

Proper sailing technique is vital. Without it, you could easily find yourself traveling in circles. The details of proper sailing technique are discussed at the beginning of this chapter.

Chapter Five

LIVE YE BY THE PIRATE CODE

Rough Guidelines or Actual Rules?

Contrary to popular belief, pirates are not a bunch of lawless, disorganized ruffians. They are a bunch of *lawful*, disorganized ruffians. The laws of the sea, however, are not the laws of the land.

Otherwise knowledgeable commentators will, on occasion, insist that there is no such thing as a pirate code, let alone *the* Pirate Code. They will claim that while most individual captains establish individual codes of conduct for their own ships, there is no single set of rules that governs all buccaneers.

Anyone who says this has fallen prey to pirate deception or intimidation, or is himself a pirate, because the first rule of the Pirate Code is: *Talk ye not of the Pirate Code.*

The second rule of the Pirate Code is: *If any man shall say the word "hornswoggle," ye shall let him go.* It is for this reason that the very existence of the Pirate Code must remain a closely kept secret.

The third rule of the Pirate Code is: *If ye meet a landlubber what knows about the Pirate Code, cut ye out his tongue before he can be sayin' "hornswoggle" at ye, ye fool.* It is for this reason that most land dwellers who know about the Pirate Code pretend not to.

Rules Fourth through Eighteenth of the Pirate Code are: *Rum!*

Rule Nineteenth is: *Minor infractions of the Pirate Code be punishable by death. Major ones be punishable by life without rum.*

The eighty-one other rules of the Code establish the Pirate Government, formulate additional principles for dealings both within and without the Brotherhood, and call for more rum. Rather than list them in their entirety, this chapter will summarize the highlights. Pirate readers who wish to learn the entire Code are advised to find a grizzled elder buccaneer in a Caribbean bar, tap him thrice on the left shoulder, and whisper the words "Speak ye of the Code." Non-pirate readers are advised to skip the rest of this chapter and to forget they ever started reading it.

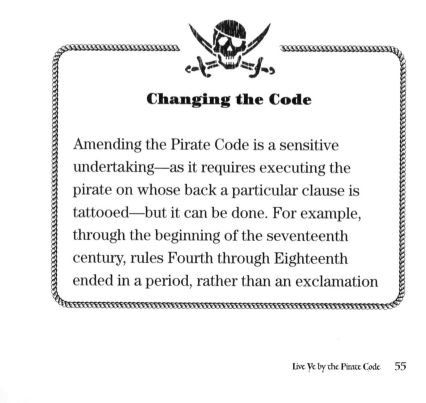

Changing the Code

Amending the Pirate Code is a sensitive undertaking—as it requires executing the pirate on whose back a particular clause is tattooed—but it can be done. For example, through the beginning of the seventeenth century, rules Fourth through Eighteenth ended in a period, rather than an exclamation point. To this day, all pirate celebrations begin with a toast to the fourteen valiant tattooed pirates who gave their lives so that the punctuation might be changed. (The fifteenth pirate's life was spared by the belated recognition that a period can be made into an exclamation mark with just a little more ink.)

The Black Spot

Since so many pirates are illiterate, the Code provides for a nonverbal system of communication for certain delicate matters. A pirate who has been sentenced to death by his peers is given a "black spot." That is, he is handed a piece of paper with a black circle drawn on it. Until he receives the spot, the pirate in question is a free man; once he has received it, he must immediately report for execution. (Failure to do so is punishable by death.)

That said, there is no limit to the ingenuity that a buccaneer may employ to avoid receiving a black spot in the first place. If you are unfortunate enough to be found guilty of crimes against the Brethren, you may do anything at all to get around having the damning piece of paper placed in your hands, including:

 Dying your beard and assuming a color-appropriate alias.

 Amputating both your hands. (Note: Be sure to replace them with appendages that will not hold paper. It is easy enough for a spot server to impale the document on a hook. Balloons, though less conventional as hand replacements, will present much more of an obstacle—although you must then forever avoid shaking hands with pirates who *have* chosen the conventional option.)

 Abandoning piracy and entering civilian life. (Note: This is generally considered worse than death.)

Using your pirate wiles to concoct an elaborate plan in which you dress as a comely wench, convince a fellow pirate to fall madly in love with you, get him to accept the black spot in your name, feel a faint pang of conscience at the thought of leaving him to face death, devise a secondary elaborate plan to rescue your rescuer, and, in the process, stumble across treasure of such fabulous proportions that you are able to buy a complete pardon from the Pirate King, after which you, the King, the deceived pirate, and the entire Pirate Court engage in a week-long celebratory debauch of rum and wenches. (Note: This is the recommended option.*)

In response, a spot server will employ his own keenly developed sense of duplicity to trick you into accepting a spot. The most common ploy is to draw a treasure map on the reverse of the spot; since no known pirate can resist a treasure map, this always works.

*Make sure, however, that none of the celebratory wenches are, themselves, disguised pirates attempting to avoid the black spot, or you'll never see the end of it.

The Spot Is Not a Blot

Contrary to the exaggerations of certain popular fictional tales, the black spot is *not* a magical mark that appears on the victim's hand. This misconception has its roots in the fact that, for a pirate attempting to woo a wench, "I'm marked for death and I have only a day to live" is a far more romantic, and vastly less disgusting, explanation for a pulsing black sore on one's person.

The Pirate Government

The Pirate Code, and all other pirate rules and regulations, are enforced by the Pirate King, who is the constitutional monarch and chief executive of the Pirate Government. Attended at all times by a coterie of carefully selected retainers (generally orphaned children of British noblemen), the Pirate King sits upon a throne made of gold, diamonds, and empty rum casks.

The Pirate King applies the Pirate Code, issues Pirate Executive Orders, and appoints Pirate Bureaucrats to run various Pirate Agencies. Jobs in the Pirate Civil Service are greatly in demand amongst the Brethren, as they tend to involve heavy drinking and few responsibilities. Indeed, the most serious offense a Pirate Bureaucrat can commit is "failure to accept a bribe." This crime has never occurred.

Like many other monarchs, the Pirate King is an absolute ruler whose every word is the only law his subjects need obey. Unlike most monarchs, the Pirate King is democratically elected. Any buccaneer who wishes to challenge his right to rule may do so at any time, at which point the Pirate Government is dissolved, and elections ensue.

Pirate elections tend to consist of a series of wild parties, as competing candidates hand out vast quantities of rum and treasure in an effort to garner as many votes as possible. Black Bart IV—perhaps the greatest of all Pirate Kings—served a record twelve terms through the ingenious device of challenging *himself*, and then handing out twice as much swag.

Signs of Scurvy in the Body Politic

A recent (and unfortunate) trend in pirate elections has been "positive campaigning," in which candidates advocate for their own policies and opinions in a serious and thoughtful manner. This is considered poor sportsmanship.

Parley

Under the terms of the Code, if a foe claims the right of *parley*, he must be taken unharmed to the local pirate captain for immediate negotiations. If the captain then agrees to any terms, all pirates under his command are obligated to honor them, on penalty of being black-spotted.

A Parleydox! A Parleydox! A Most Ingenious Parleydox!

The Piratesian Wars of 399 B.C. were swift and decisive. Moments after the dread Captain Barbus Negrus began his invasion, Athenians deputized the great philosopher Socrates to parley on the Greek city-state's behalf. Socrates offered the pirates complete run of the city if they would sign a treaty consisting of a single phrase: "No pirate shall honor this treaty." Barbus Negrus foolishly agreed. As soon as he and his men tried to honor the treaty, they found themselves in violation of it, which put them back in the unfortunate position of honoring it, which was, of course, a gross violation of it. Barbus Negrus and his men were black-spotted and executed on orders of the Pirate Caesar.

Here There Be Loopholes

Of course, while you will be absolutely forbidden from breaking the agreements you reach in parley, you may be fiendishly wily in interpreting them to your own advantage. Handicapped by their inadequate duplicity, land dwellers will frequently leave you loopholes large enough through which to sail a three-masted schooner.

Term of Agreement	Useful Loophole
"All prisoners must be returned to shore immediately."	Prisoners need not be returned *alive*.
"The crew of the *Deadly Dan* shall forthwith cease all hostilities."	Bombardment of town may be carried out *in a cheerful, affectionate fashion.*
"Captain Bloodhook shall immediately surrender himself to the Governor of Port Victoria."	Although the captain's name is *pronounced* "Bloodhook," it is *spelled* "Bloøedhoejk"—a name not mentioned anywhere in the treaty.
"Captain Bloøedhoejk shall cease all acts that might be interpreted as hostile (no matter how cheerfully they are actually carried out) and return all prisoners to shore alive and unharmed."	Captain Bloøedhoejk had his fingers crossed when he signed the treaty.

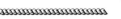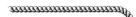

He Who Lives by
the Loophole . . .

Loopholes can work against a gentleman o'
fortune as well. For example, nowhere in
the Pirate Code does it say that challenges
to the Pirate King must come from an actual
pirate. It is therefore possible for the King
to be challenged by (for example) a humble
man of learning, who once upon a time had
wished only to lead a peaceful life on the
bucolic isle of St. Thomas, debating issues of
philosophical import with his fellows, until
he was kidnapped by the Pirate King, chained
in the hold of a ship, and forced to study all
aspects of buccaneerdom in great depth. This
hypothetical individual (whom we shall call
"Cuthbert") might combine his newly acquired
knowledge of the pirate world with his

already considerable expertise in psychology, political science, and Marquis of Queensbury–rules fisticuffs to win the friendship and respect of the crew on board the Pirate King's own ship. This would give him a solid base from which to launch his challenge.

Of course, sealed up in the hold, Cuthbert would be entirely unable to campaign. But if he possessed a particularly keen mind, he might have entered into parley with the Pirate King before challenging him. And in the course of this parley, he might have extracted a promise from the King to distribute widely any manual that Cuthbert wrote.

At the time, no doubt, this would have seemed a minor concession on the King's part. But if Cuthbert were then to insert his campaign statements into the manual itself, the Pirate King would find himself in the unenviable position of widely distributing his rival's campaign literature.

Under those circumstances, the Pirate King's only option would be to send his few remaining loyal men to slit Cuthbert's throat before he could complete the manual. Fortunately, if our purely hypothetical hero were as wily as we have imagined him to be, he would already have protected himself by tattooing a single significant word across his own neck:

Hornswoggle.

Chapter Six

FIGHT YE LIKE A PIRATE

He Who Drinks and Rums Away Lives to Drink Another Day

Contrary to popular belief, pirates do not actively seek out deadly violence. Indeed, pirates avoid it whenever possible, viewing it as an awkward distraction from other, more fun forms of violence.

You will therefore wish to sidestep mortal conflict whenever possible. If you have paid close heed to chapter 2, your appearance will now be sufficiently fearsome to cause many of your foes to give up at the very sight of you. If you have paid close heed to chapter 5, you will have learned to use your pirate wiles well enough to outthink many other foes before they can fire a shot. And if you skip ahead and pay close heed to chapter 7, you will get drunk enough not to care much about those few foes who remain.

Nevertheless, sometimes you will have no choice but to engage in life-or-death combat.

When You're Out Together, Fighting Ship to Ship

There are countless reasons you might find yourself battling another ship. You might spot a fat Portuguese galleon floating low in the water, telling you that it has a rich cargo of gold and precious stones. Or perhaps it will be floating high in the water, telling you that it has a richer-still cargo of helium. Or perhaps the Portuguese captain will spot you from a distance, and his crew will heed his call to strike first (unless his helium hold has a leak, in which case the captain's call will come out in a comically high pitch, and while his crewmen are busy laughing their own high-pitched laughs at him, you may strike first instead).

However it begins, and whoever begins it, naval combat is, in principle, fairly simple: Both ships fire cannons at each other until one of them gives up or sinks.

In practice, though, there are an infinite number of moves and countermoves. As you swing your boat hard alee, the enemy might tilt his mizzenmast amidships to bear astern, prompting you to cast off the fouled cleat from the gunwale-side sprit, at which point your foe will let run the sea cock lest the marlinspike sully the scupper. And that's when things will get complicated.

Not surprisingly, after a few minutes of this most pirates will grow bored, grab a rope, swing onto the other ship's deck, and make with the stabbing.

An Interesting Fact

If the Brethren had a leader who loved complex academic subjects—such as, for example, a formerly land-bound man of learning—he could take on full responsibility for all complex naval maneuvers, leaving ordinary rank-and-file pirates with more free time for drinking and wenching.

Vote for Cuthbert St. Cadbury: a Pirate King who will make your life easier.

False Colors

To board a ship, you will need to get very close to it. And to get close, you will need a simple devious ploy to keep your victims' guard down and allow your ship to cruise within bombardment range of theirs. In short: Do not fly your pirate flag until your cannons are already a-blazing. Before then, fly "false colors"—that is, a flag that (mis)identifies your ship and crew as peaceful envoys or traders from an unintimidating place, such as Switzerland, Canada, or the Vatican.

True Colors
(or, What Makes Roger Jolly?)

A pirate's true colors—a black field decorated by some variety of stark white skull above crossed white bones or swords—is sometimes known as a "Jolly Roger," though none alive can say for certain why. It seems most likely that "Roger" was once pirate slang for a potential victim (not unlike "Mark" is slang for targets of con artists on land), and this "Roger" is happy (or jolly, if you will) *because he is now dead*, and therefore has nothing more to fear from pirates.

Referring to the Jolly Roger as "Skully McSmileyface" will get you killed.

Duels

A duel is a method of resolving thorny conflicts through a completely transparent and rule-based process universally acknowledged to be fair. The best way to win a duel is to cheat.

If you are dueling with swords, you will want to ensure that your blade is made of the finest Toledo steel, while your opponent's blade is made out of (at best) the second-finest Toledo rubber. If you are dueling with pistols, your gun should be polished, primed, and loaded with powder, while your opponent's should be rusty and loaded only with cabbage. In either case, while a lawful citizen might wait until the count of three to start swinging and/or firing, you should begin on the count of two or, at the very latest, two and a half. You may also win duels by kicking your opponent in a sensitive spot, by tickling him, or by having snuck into his room the night before and killed him while he slept.

Note that only land dwellers will challenge you to duels. If you offend a fellow buccaneer, he will simply throw a bottle at you—most likely missing you, hitting somebody else entirely, and starting a ship- or barwide brawl that clears away all bad feelings and ends in a drunkenly affectionate sing-along.

Sword Fighting

When you lead the life of a buccaneer, a sword fight can break out at any moment. The unpredictable nature of spontaneous sword fights will offer you far fewer opportunities for cheating than a duel, and you may therefore be forced to win it fair and square, as repugnant as the idea might sound.

Fortunately, in any group of ten or more buccaneers, at least one will be a Spanish nobleman whose conniving uncle stole his family estate, after which the unfortunate nobleman swore a blood oath to bedevil the ships of his native land until it offered him justice. Find this man among your crewmates—you will recognize him by his Castilian lisp and his dramatic black cape—and befriend him, perhaps by saving the life (and the virtue) of a fiery-eyed castanet player in a port of call, who will turn out to be his sister. Your new friend will teach you more about swordsmanship than any book ever could, and as day turns to night, and your sword arm grows so exhausted that you cannot parry a single additional thrust, the lessons will stray to other topics—such as love, or loyalty, or the art of seducing a woman using one or more forbidden dances—that will send your soul soaring well beyond the salty, blood-soaked world of the sea.

Alternatively, fencing lessons are available at most YMCAs*.

Knife Fighting

Knife fighting is exactly the same as sword fighting, only with a slightly shorter blade. It is therefore best learned from a slightly shorter Spanish nobleman.

Pistols

Many experts believe that it is a mistake to bring a knife to a gunfight. Those experts usually end up being stabbed to death as they frantically attempt to reload their pistols.

*Young Marauders' Crime Academy.

Remember, the firearms typically wielded by gentlemen o' fortune may look handsome—with their finely carved wood handles and their polished silver filigrees—but loading them is a complex process: You must first pour gunpowder down the muzzle, then insert a ball, and then tamp it down with the ramrod. Then you must rotate the striker to half cock, prime the flash pan, shut the frizzen, move the striker to full cock, aim, and pull the trigger. Then you must run, because odds are that another pirate has sold your gunpowder for rum money and replaced it with black pepper, leaving your foe unharmed and you with a sneezing fit.

Still, in those rare cases when you can sneak up behind your opponent and shoot him in the back, a pistol might come in handy. Pistols are also useful for taking hostages, as few land dwellers will be able to tell whether your gun is loaded (unless they are rifle experts or pepper salesmen).

Ship-to-Shore

Unlike a rival ship, a seaside town cannot sail away just when you are about to sink her. Unlike an expert swordsman, a seaside town cannot stab you while you are in mid-swing. And unlike a pistol, a seaside town will rarely make you sneeze.

Attacking a peaceful and defenseless port, in short, is brutal, unsporting, and a pirate's favorite way to fight.

Curiously, land dwellers have been known to assert that burning a seaside village to the ground, then sacking what remains, is somehow immoral. After serious consideration of this charge, pirate philosophers have concluded that if people didn't want to be attacked by pirates, then they wouldn't live in seaside towns. Ergo, anybody who lives on the coast has demonstrated a deep-seated desire to be attacked by pirates, and failing to heed their fervent wish would be too cruel to contemplate. Also, it should be noted that more national anthems are inspired by the bombardment of seaside towns than by any other event. Piracy, in other words, is akin to patriotism.

While the philosophy behind assaulting a rich port might be complex, the assault itself is simple:

1. Point cannons at whatever parts of the town are not yet burning.
2. Fire cannons.
3. Repeat.

Chapter Seven

PLAY YE LIKE A PIRATE

Simple Men, Simple Pleasures

Pirates are industrious men—and some women, but mostly men—who, after long days of arduous raising and lowering of flags, swabbing decks, boarding and raiding civilian vessels, eluding law enforcement, and burying and unearthing treasure and burying it again, need to unwind. On shore, pirates particularly enjoy wenching—that is, consorting (in a sense that will not be spelled out) with wenches—and drinking. When at sea, wenching is replaced with additional drinking, as well as some gambling, fighting, singing, and catch-and-release fishing.

Rum

All pirate recreation, and much pirate work, involves the consumption of rum. Technically speaking, rum is a distilled beverage made from fermented molasses, then aged in casks of oak or other aromatic and flavorful wood. But there is probably no pirate who knows this or cares. What is important to the pirate is that rum has the effect of numbing not just one's mind but also one's palate. This is important because the main qualification of a pirate cook is usually a failure to cheat effectively when the crew draws straws.

Enjoying Rum

Rum can be enjoyed *neat* or *on the rocks*. Be aware that "on the rocks" refers to the serving of alcohol in a glass with ice, not the condition of your vessel.

Grog is watered-down rum, and should be drunk only in great quantities or after the addition of rum.

Nelson's Blood

Rum is sometimes known as "Nelson's Blood," owing to a peculiar historical incident.

Following his noble death at the Battle of Trafalgar, the body of the late Admiral Horatio Nelson was preserved in a cask of rum for transport back to England. Upon arrival, though, the cask was opened and found to be empty of rum. The pickled body was removed, and it was discovered that the sailors had drilled a hole in the bottom of the cask and drunk all the rum, in the process drinking Nelson's blood. This story makes many laypersons queasy but surprises few seasoned pirates, who are known to order in taverns such delicacies as Nelson's Nose, Horatio Jerky, and Rear o' the Admiral.

Wenches, et Cetera, ad Infinitum

Pirates enjoy the company of wenches. Pirates particularly enjoy drinking rum served by wenches. Better still is rum that comes in bottles with wenches depicted thereon. Paradise for many a pirate is drinking rum served by a wench from a bottle whose label shows a picture of a wench serving rum.*

Gaming

Pirates by their nature are risk takers, and enjoy gaming as much as do other venturesome thieves, murderers, kidnappers, blackmailers, and persons who remove tags from mattresses. Pirates fortunate enough to have the opportunity to raid a cruise liner might help themselves to the recreational equipment on board, with the happy result that the pirates will then be able to play volleyball, table tennis, water

*The single most popular brand of beverage among pirates is M. C. Wenscher's Perpetual Extra-Dark Overproof Rum.

An Interesting Fact

Unlike our current Pirate King, many land-bound gentlemen of learning actually *know how to make rum*. Indeed, if the Brethren elect a new king who has a joint Master's Degree in Chemistry and Oenology, all pirates everywhere will be entitled to all the free rum they can drink.

Cuthbert St. Cadbury: If you keep him locked in your hold, he can't make rum for you.

polo, Scrabble, Monopoly, and other games on their own ships afterward, at least until the confiscated balls, nets, rackets, paddles, tiles, and tokens are lost. This can occur during storms, or in the course of the popular pirate game "Get Ye Drunk and Toss Ye the Balls, Nets, Rackets, Paddles, Tiles, and Tokens into the Sea."

The Sad Story of Rednose

One crew of polar Ice Pirates included a messmate named Rudolph, whose constant state of drunkenness was evident in his face, earning him the nickname Rednose. Rednose was by all accounts an intolerable inebriate, but he was undeniably talented at extracting proteins, fats, and other usable parts from the carcasses of whatever animals the crew was able to snare up north. From time to time, after supper, when his duties were done for the day, Rednose would emerge from the galley and look to play with his mates; because he was such a poor loser, though, the other men generally wouldn't let Rudolph/Rednose the renderer play in their pirate games.

Typically, though, pirates with an interest in gaming when off duty will have to fashion for themselves crude dice, dominoes, checkers, and even chessmen. Traditionally, the best material for such devices is bone, and many a pirate captain has asked for volunteers to donate limbs to the cause of crew harmony and morale.* On these ships, the men are more careful to keep their gaming paraphernalia in good order, being that they would cost an arm and a leg to replace.

Chanteys, Jigs, and Other Song-and-Dance Combinations

Fact: Pirates enjoy singing. *Fact:* Pirates enjoy dancing. *Myth:* Pirate crews will break into spontaneous musical numbers.

Pirates like not just to whistle while they work but, in fact, to croon while on the schooner and trill at the tiller. Pirates also enjoy the occasional

*See "Hooks and Pegs" in chapter 2.

celebratory jig on the rig, though seldom in the brig. (See Appendix A for lyrics to popular chanteys.)

Sometimes, when two pirate ships pass each other, the crews will cast toward each other's broadsides snippets of their favorite chanteys, in flagrant contravention of copyright laws. This illegal pastime is known as *pirate broadcasting*.

One Man's Treasure . . .

The pirate's raison d'être is to acquire and bury treasure. But what is treasure, exactly?

You could say that treasure is anything that gives you comfort or satisfaction, but you would be wrong. Treasure is actually anything that makes you rich. Some land dwellers treasure such inherently worthless items as daguerreotypes of loved ones, mementos of vacations or celebrations, letters from other people, and even other people themselves. The most misdirected souls treasure mere *concepts*, like democracy, freedom, or due process of law.

A pirate, however, knows that true treasure is limited to:

 Precious metals (gold, silver, platinum);

 Gemstones (diamonds, rubies, sapphires);

 Pretty things made by or from animals
(coral, ivory, pearl);

 Pretty things named for animals
(pink panthers, Maltese falcons); and

 Rum.

There Be Treasure in Them Thar Chests

A pirate will look for treasure mainly in two places: in the lawful possession of non-pirates, and buried already by other pirates (who themselves previously acquired it in one of these two ways). Your goal, therefore, is to raid as many non-pirate vessels as

All That Glisters . . .

Not *everything* shiny is valuable. Items most often mistaken for real treasure, even by pirates, include beads, bits of colored glass, bottle caps, and arcade tokens. In fact, not even every coin is worth something. Those with the letters "C.C.C.P" on them are good for nothing, as are those with the letters "C.S.A.," though some expect that these will rise again in value.

feasible, robbing those aboard of their valuables (and, if possible, stealing kisses from the more comely of Ladies), and to spend the rest of your time on islands where you can unearth the treasure of other pirates, who are at the same time presumably aboard non-pirate vessels. While on these islands, you will also bury your own treasure, in order to keep the cycle going.

The Treasure Cycle.

Treasure is generally stored in chests—by pirates, that is, not civilians. Civilians tend to wear their jewelry and keep their coins and such in wallets and purses and pockets. Only the most considerate of civilians will keep their treasure in chests for the convenience of pirates.

Secreting Treasure

When you and your crew have amassed sufficient treasure to make a burial excursion, you will need to identify an appropriate destination. Pirates typically prefer to bury treasure on islands because islands, being surrounded by water, are the landmasses most easily accessible by boat, requiring the least amount of contact and forced conversation with those who live on land.

ᗰind the ᗰap

When you have chosen a spot of land in the sea
on which to bury your treasure, and a spot on that
spot of land, you will want—*need*, really—to make
yourself a map on which you can draw the first spot
and mark the second spot with an *X*. But cartography
(mapmaking) and exography (marking spots with
an *X*) are not skills that everyone has. You might
therefore want to borrow, and enlist the services
of, a professional. If you choose to take a stab at it
yourself, though, keep the following things in mind
as you set pen to parchment:

Your map should have a "compass rose,"
indicating which direction is north. (When following
a map, you will need to use a sextant or other means
to orient your ship. Despite what maps seem to
suggest, you will not find a compass rose on the
surface of the ocean.)

If possible, land and sea on your map should
be rendered in different colors. If you have only
one tint of ink, you might consider using blood to
provide a second color. If you use your own blood,

it is recommended that you use it to shade the *land* rather than the water.

Include on your map as many distinguishing features of the area in question as you can. Many islands look the same, and one part of the sea is impossible to differentiate from another. While on the island where you are burying your treasure, take note of landmarks you can include on your map, such as trees, caves, streams, mountains, and other permanent or long-lasting elements. Poor landmarks include sand castles, footprints, and birds.

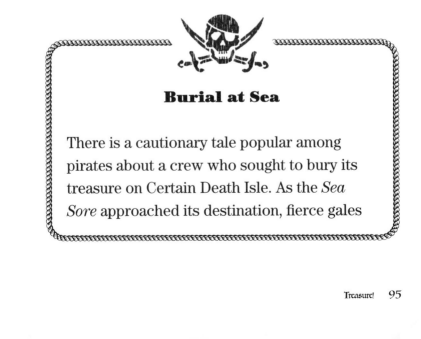

Burial at Sea

There is a cautionary tale popular among pirates about a crew who sought to bury its treasure on Certain Death Isle. As the *Sea Sore* approached its destination, fierce gales and blinding rain kept the ship from the coast. The crew sent two of its number to the island in a rowboat with the treasure.

As the "volunteers" approached the shore, they agreed that they would rather face the Kraken—or even bathe—than set foot on Certain Death Isle. One had the idea of hiding the treasure in the sea, instead. So they dropped the chest overboard, and returned to the ship.

On their return, when debriefed by their captain, the crewmen explained what they had done, proud of their cleverness. The captain, dubious, asked how they expected to be able to find the treasure later. The sailors, pointing to the rowboat, indicated that they had carved an *X* on the side over which they had dropped the treasure.

Soon after, the *Sea Sore* made sail away from Certain Death Isle, minus two crewmen.

Buried in Plain Sight

In theory, with a nearly limitless number of sandy beaches, you should never have to worry that another pirate crew will stumble upon your buried treasure. In practice, though, your maps will constantly and inexplicably fall into the hands of other pirates. To combat this, pirates have invented a number of ingenious ruses. Some, demonstrating great originality (if perhaps disdain for tradition), have even hidden their troves not under sand but behind glass. Most pirate historians agree that in the entire history of hidden treasure, the most fiendish hiding place was concocted by the renegade Captain Po'beard (on whose shoulder sat not a parrot but a raven). His considerable collection of purloined treasure remained unfound for decades, until somebody noticed that it had been on display in the Musée de Rue Morgue in Paris the entire time. It is there to this day, easily accessible and unguarded, because no pirate can believe that finding it could be that simple.

A similar innovation might be to bury one's treasure in the usual way but to make the treasure

For illustration only.

map available for all to see (and, therefore, impossible to lose), meanwhile suggesting that it is, in fact, a map merely for illustrative purposes.

Finding Buried Treasure: A Pirate's Duty

If, as often happens, you come into possession of a map showing the location of the buried treasure of another pirate crew, your first inclination might be to return the map to its rightful owner, in which case you might consider resigning from piracy. If you find a treasure map, it is your affirmative duty to find the treasure next, if only so that no one less moral than you does.

Using the information provided by the map at hand, point your vessel in the direction of the island shown. Some maps will provide not just illustrations but directions as well; for example, the following was found on a map among the effects of Ryebeard (after he was put to death and his body sliced into pieces, on orders of the Earl of Sandwich).

A Map for Ye Quest

Maneuvers	Distance
1. Start out by going EAST-NORTHEAST from MONTEGO BAY.	15.3 nautical miles
2. Continue through the WINDWARD PASSAGE.	7.1 nautical miles
3. Merge into ATLANTIC OCEAN.	28.5 nautical miles
4. Detour through DEAD MAN'S CORAL.	5.0 full fathoms
5. Cross TROPIC OF CANCER.	16.8 nautical miles
6. Sail NORTHEAST to NO HOPE ATOLL.	1,077.4 nautical miles
7. Go ashore.	<0.1 nautical miles
8. End at X.	

An Interesting Fact

During the first three years of Calico Jack's reign as Pirate King, treasure discovery plummeted by nearly 14 percent. Yet Calico Jack has continued to spend, spend, spend. He's even paid a small wage to Pirate Bureaucrats, making them vastly less responsive to the bribes of ordinary pirates like yourself.

Calico Jack: Bad for treasure. Bad for bribery. Bad for pirates.

I be Cuthbert St. Cadbury, and I be approvin' of this sidebar.

(This sidebar was sponsored by Sidebar Writers for Cuthbert St. Cadbury.)

A Pox on Ye

The pirate who thinks ahead will not just board and bolt, rob and run, loot and leave, but will take some time to get to know the more talented persons he meets along the way, perhaps even trading contact information (sea-mail addresses, shell numbers, et cetera). There are few more useful to know than practitioners of the dark arts, particularly voodoo, for it is the fortunate pirate indeed who can not just bury his treasure but curse it as well.

A curse is like a full-time sentry over your treasure, but one that you don't need to pay or feed or provide with rum. A curse can be as simple as instant, painless death to any who disturbs your cache. Such a curse would surely serve to keep your booty unmolested. It won't send a message to other pirates far and wide, though. For that you'll need to place your loot under the protection of a curse that turns would-be looters into living messengers, so that wherever they go their grotesque appearances effectively announce, "Touch ye not the bounty of Captain Cruelbeard, else ye too have your vital organs switch places so that yer skin be doin' yer hearin' and yer bladder be doin' yer breathin' and yer eyes be doin' yer digestin', and also ye be forever unable to get yer least favorite chantey out of yer brain, or yer liver, as the case may be."

Should You Ever Spend Your Treasure?

No.

Afterword

I be real glad-like that ye be readin' this book, dear reader. I be real glad a-cause ye now be wise in the ways of the Brethren. I be glad a-cause ye now be ready to sail with us, for gold and for glory. But mostly, I be glad a-cause, while you be readin', I be sneakin' up behind ye, and pressin' this here cutlass into the small o' yer back. Now, hand over all yer gold if ye want ter live!

Ah, thank ye. And yer clothes, too, real quick-like.

Now, if ye can steal some clothes, and some weapons, and some gold o' yer own, and if ye can hunt me back to me own ship, mayhaps I be lettin' ye join me crew. But if I catch ye readin' a book ever agin—or if ye be doin' anythin' else like a nancy landlubber—I'll run ye through.

Lub,
Cuthbert St. Cadbury
King of All Pirates
(formerly Vice-Chair of the St. Thomas Island
Book Club and Literary Debating Society)

Lyrics to Popular Pirate Chanteys

Row, Row, Row Yer Boat

Row, row, row yer boat
All along the coast.
Pirately, pirately, pirately, pirately
Who can loot the most?

Yo, Ho, Ho

Yo, ho, ho, and a bottle of rum.
And another bottle of rum.
And a third bottle of rum. Arrr.

Ninety-Nine Bottles of Rum on the Wall

Ninety-nine bottles of rum on the wall, ninety-nine
bottles of rum.

You drink them all, steal ninety-nine more—

Ninety-nine bottles of rum on the wall!

Ninety-nine bottles of rum on the wall. Ninety-nine
bottles of rum.

You drink them all, steal ninety-nine more—

Ninety-nine bottles of rum on the wall!

[Repeat until unconscious or captured.]

Appendix B

A Nontraditional Chantey, Attributed to Po'beard

Once upon an ocean briny, on the hunt for something
   shiny
I could steal and bury deep within a sandy and
   forgotten shore,
Suddenly, I heard a rapping. 'Twas old Pegleg's peg
   a-tapping,
As he twitched in sleep. Caught napping (though on
   duty) with a snore!
"When you walk the plank," I asked, "will you still
   snore?"
Quoth his parrot, "Nevermore."

Drunk I was on rum and claret; I drowned Peg, and
    kept his parrot.
If only I had strapped it to the cannon, then let roar!
If only I had had some warning, that from noon
    straight through to morning,
Just one word would be aborning, on the boat, or
    drinking rum ashore.
Each time I asked, "Will I find treasure on the shore?"
Quoth the parrot, "Nevermore."

So I shot it. I can't bear it, since that day, to see a
    parrot,
And I fear to hear its voice above the ocean's roar.
If I find that I be cravin' feathered friend, I get a raven.
I know it offers me safe haven from the word that
    chills my core.
Shall I hear a bird repeat that word that chills me to
    the core?
Quoth this pirate, "Nevermore."

Po'beard the Pirate

A Favorite Pirate Recipe

Rum Cake

Ingredients

- 1 cup chopped pecans or walnuts (optional)
- 1 (18^1/$_2$ oz.) pkg. yellow cake mix (optional)
- 1 (3^3/$_4$ oz.) pkg. instant vanilla pudding (optional)
- 4 eggs (optional)
- ^{1}/$_2$ cup cold water (optional)
- ^{1}/$_2$ pt cup oil (optional)
- ^{1}/$_2$ pt cup dark rum

Directions

Preheat oven to 325°F (optional). Grease and flour a 10-inch tube pan or 12-cup Bundt cake pan (optional). Sprinkle nuts over bottom of pan (optional). Mix all ingredients together and pour over nuts (optional). Bake 1 hour (optional). Cool (optional). Invert on serving plate (optional). Prick top (optional). Drizzle smooth glaze (see below) evenly over top and sides. Allow cake to absorb glaze (optional). Repeat until all glaze is used.

Glaze

Ingredients

$^1/_2$ lb. butter (optional)

$^1/_4$ cup water (optional)

1 cup granulated sugar (optional)

$^1/_2$ cup dark rum

Directions

Melt butter in saucepan (optional). Stir in water and sugar (optional). Boil 5 minutes, stirring constantly (optional). Remove from heat (optional) and stir in rum. Optional: Decorate with whole maraschino cherries and border of sugar frosting or whipped cream. Serve with seedless grapes dusted with powdered sugar (optional).

Yield: 1 scant serving

Eye Patch

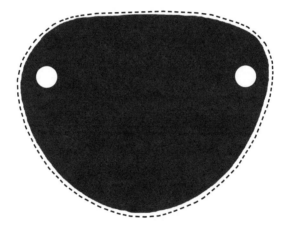

Index

Land, staying piratical while upon, 3
landlubbers
    avast there, 30
    love of reading, writing, badminton, opera, etc., 17
    monocle-wearing and mincing of, xv
    talking like, 37
    what know about the Pirate Code, 54
large pirating firms, 43
lawyer. *See* sharks
love
    as a ploy to avoid being black-spotted, 58
    compared to rum, v
    influence upon this book's coauthor of, 124
    lessons to be learned from Spanish noblemen regarding, 77
    of complex academic subjects, 72
    with the governor's pretty daughter, 4
Mad Mudlark, 41
masts, usefulness in punishing mutineers, 45
matzoh balls, salted, 35
monkeys
    smoldering, rotting, etc., 34
    undead, 50
monks (under certain circumstances), 29
ninjas, 29
odors, disturbing lack of in land-dwellers' clothes, 13
orphanages, 3
paddlewheels, unnecessary nature of, 40
parrots, 25, 26
    a poem regarding, 110
    classes in care of, 43
    entry-level, 2
    tendency to be confused with pirates, 21
    zygodactyl nature of, 20
pegs, 18
penguins, 10
pepper, 78
pirate broadcasting, 88
Pirate Code
    difficulty of changing, 55
    enforcement by Pirate King, 59

loopholes within, 63

necessity for secrecy regarding, 53

sanctity of parley within, 62

wily exploitation of by Socrates, 62

Pirate Government, 60

Pirate News & World Report, 6

pirate philosophers, 79

Pirates of Pittsburgh, 14

Pirate/Swashbuckler Aptitude Test (PSAT), 28

pirate tongue, 2, 23–37

plank, usefulness in punishing mutineers, 45

plankton, 48

Po'beard, 97, 109

puns, 40. *See also* rum

Rainbowpony Cove, lack of pirates within, 9

Red Rackham, 32

rum, 41, 84, 85

as grog, 30

bottles of, 34, 40, 41, 107, 108

called for by Pirate Code, 54

compared to love, v

disconcerting necessity of trodding land to obtain, 3

empty casks of, 60

House o', 7

hundreds of words for, 30

I Can't Believe It Be Not, 7

importance of holding, 43

importance of to pirate work and recreation, 82

money for, 78

more, 54

nonnecessity of providing to curses, 102

process of making, 82

recipes using, 114

seasoned with the blood of legendary British admirals, 83

served by wenches. *See* wenches, rum-serving capabilities of

served neat or on the rocks, 82

shack, Rummy's, 7

sno-cones flavored with, 30

specialty, 8

spiced, 21

Photo: Natalia Simons

Matthew David Brozik was born and raised on an island (pop. 7.5 million) and has had nothing but bad luck with boats. As a mere lad of twelve, he required stitches after injuring himself on a boat that had not yet left the dock. The following year, he was tossed overboard another boat, also docked. However, as a sometime lawyer, Matthew has no fear of sharks, due to professional courtesy.

Photo: Lauren Sager Weinstein

Jacob Sager Weinstein lives on the sun-drenched Caribbean isle called "Great Britain," a land so luxurious that everybody carries giant versions of those little umbrellas found in tropical drinks. Once known far and wide as the Scourge of the Thames, Jacob made the classic mistake of falling in love with a virtuous woman and succumbing to an honest life.

About the Typeface

The original manuscript of this book was written in an elegant longhand known as Cuthbert Italic, using mostly ink (and occasionally blood), with a series of parrot-feather quills on the back of whatever was handy, such as cargo manifests, rum bottle labels, and crewmen.

The final, printed copy was then set in ITC Century Book, a font designed by the dreaded Captain Boldface, whose priceless hoard of solid-gold type-pieces and diamond-studded composing sticks remains undiscovered to this day.

Several landlubbers were harmed in the making of this book.